discover calm

The easy way to a quiet mind and calm emotions.

For people with little time to spare.

Neale Daniel

First published May 2011

Rev5   June 2011

ISBN 978-1-4477-1018-9

Cover image by Federico Stevanin   at www.FreeDigitalPhotos.net

Published by Neale Daniel

www.NealeDaniel.com

Email neale@nealedaniel.com

Printed by Lulu

www.lulu.com

To Jillian

Acknowledgements

Many thanks to my mentor Dave Lucas for getting me started and Soo Vinnicombe my editor for turning an idea into a book.

Contents

Introduction

Who is this book for?
If you feel your life is becoming too hectic or your mind never ceases in its chattering. If you sometimes experience agitation, sadness, fear or anger then this guide can help you bring about a lighter, easier way of living by offering a gentle way to change your approach to everyday life.

How does it work?
It is about re-connecting with yourself and becoming more aware of the world around you and finding calmness within. This is a collection of simple approaches that you can try out, helping you find calm in your daily life. Different methods work for different people, so this book gives you a chance to try lots of alternative approaches and discover the ones that work best for you.

Why have I written this?
I have spent years experimenting with various relaxation techniques in an effort to calm my chattering mind which often kept me awake at night. Simple frustrations used to lead to feelings of anger which made me uncomfortable with myself. Many of the classic relaxation approaches were incompatible with my busy life, but I did find some simple methods that worked. This book is a collection of other author's techniques' and some of my own – almost a taster course of what is available.

What is the programme?

The programme of weekly tasks follows 8 simple stages:

1 Unburdening your busy mind
2 Simple ways of distracting your mind from its chatter
3 Using your wider world as a distraction
4 Creating opportunities to rest your mind
5 Becoming aware of your emotions
6 Simple ways of calming your emotions
7 Playtime for the mind
8 Review

We begin by unburdening your busy mind, and then look at different ways of distracting your mind from its chattering thoughts. The distraction exercises start by simply becoming aware of yourself physically, and then of your place in the world. They are about grounding yourself and finding a point of reference in your life, that you can return to when the going gets tough. We then look at approaches that give your mind a rest.

Next you will begin to listen to the chatter of your mind, becoming aware of your emotions, observing them as they happen. With practice this has the gentle effect of calming your reactions to situations. We also introduce some techniques to further calm your emotions.

We finish on a lighter note with some techniques to provide your mind with some play time.

How to read the book

The book is arranged as a step by step guide, with one simple exercise each week. Reading the instructions at the beginning of the week and then attempting the tasks described during the following weekdays. Our aim is to find calmness in your life, so what better way to start than reading the book very slowly over many months. Reading in a conventional way from cover to cover is unlikely to be of much help, this is very much a practical experience and all the benefits come from practising the daily tasks.

None of the exercises are demanding or occupy lots of your time. Some can be quite challenging or seem pointless at first, but please just give them a go. What have you to lose? You may be surprised. At the end of each chapter we will visit a 'workshop' of your choice, to practice some of the techniques we have learnt. An ideal location is your regular supermarket visit.

The knack is to get into the regular habit of snatching a few seconds or minutes here and there from your daily routine for each exercise.

Your personal challenge is to see if you can give yourself a little space each day to let your mind take a rest, this can bring about a lighter happier way of living. But above all, try to have some fun doing it.

Summary of the weekly activities

The week can be split into three brief sessions.

- Day 1   Read about the week's technique (few minutes)
- Days 2-6   Practice the daily tasks (grab odd moments)
- Day 7   Review the week & make notes (few minutes)

At the end of each chapter we also visit the supermarket 'workshop'.

How do I remember to be calm?

The key to achieving calm is to get into the habit of carrying out these tasks on a regular basis during your day. The weekly tasks only take a few moments of your time, but one of the difficulties of incorporating them into your daily life is remembering to do them during the first few weeks. One possible approach is to use visual reminders to prompt you to complete a daily task. Once you are in the habit of completing the tasks, you will no longer need these visual reminders.

You can make your own reminders or cut the pictures from the back of the book. Leave the pictures in places that you will discover during your normal working day. For example in your wallet, purse or perhaps in a drawer that you open daily. When you see the cards let them act as a reminder for you to carry out your weekly calming exercise.

The reminders do not have to mean anything to anyone but you.

Making notes:

You can use this book as a notebook. A space has been left after each exercise for making notes, this can be very helpful for reviewing your progress as you work through the various exercises.

Supermarket workshops:
At the end of each chapter we will visit a 'workshop' to practice the weekly exercises. Your 'workshop' needs to be a place where you are challenged emotionally, but still gives you the opportunity to safely practice some of the exercises. For example it could be family visits, the workplace or the supermarket. The supermarket is ideal because you are only there for a short period, just enough time to try out some of the techniques. If things don't work out, you can just walk away which could be difficult in the work place.

Before you progress any further, you need to choose an appropriate location for your workshop. For the purposes of this book I will use the Supermarket, because it is ideally suited, having all the key features that we require:

- o   Regular visits.
- o   Short duration.
- o   Emotionally challenging environment.
- o   Opportunities to meet people who may annoy you.
- o   A place where you can be relatively anonymous.

On a practical note:
Don't worry about sticking to the schedule, it is just a guideline. If something works well for you, then why not do it for a few weeks. Also, if you find you are getting no benefit from a technique, just move onto the next. Remember, out of all the different techniques in this book, you only need to discover a couple that work well for you.

Chapter 1   Unburdening your mind

We begin by finding ways to quickly unburden your mind and give it less work to do. If we take the very simplistic analogy of the brain as a muscle, then it is great to exercise a muscle but you need to give it some time to rest and repair, otherwise you will start to develop injuries over the longer term. We shall begin by just reducing the amount of hard exercise that our mind does, with the aim over future weeks of giving your thinking mind progressively more opportunities to rest. By reducing the long term stress on your mind we may avoid some of the potential mental health issues.

First week   *Make lists*

Our minds flow with an incessant stream of busy thoughts for most of the day, one thing that contributes to this is repetitive thoughts about the things that we need to do. Offloading those jobs that must be done onto paper can release quite a weight from your mind.

Find a pen, paper and create two lists; a short list of priority tasks that you really must do immediately and a long list of all those tasks that should be done at some point in the future, if only you had the time. Make the low priority list as long as you like, adding any obscure idea, or aspiration that enters your mind.

Daily tasks

Over the following days and weeks, keep adding new items to your lists as they occur to you. Unburden your mind and move them directly to your lists. If tasks are complete then cross them off the list.

List rules:

1. If items remain on the short priority list for weeks then move them onto the less urgent list. They can't really be all that urgent.
2. Attempt the tasks on the priority list first.

Now PAUSE Reading

After a week of using your lists has passed.
Resume reading

Personal notes

What worked well for you?

What did you discover?

How did this make you feel?

End of week review

Do you find that you are doing the more interesting or easy tasks from the less urgent list rather than the tedious or dull ones from your priority list? If so then the priority items are still nagging you and you are gaining no benefit from the lists. It requires self discipline to complete the dull urgent tasks. Try to make the lists a part of your daily life, and consider giving yourself a treat as a reward when you complete a dull priority task. Continue to use your lists over the coming weeks.

There will be an interesting twist in the way we use the lists in a few weeks time.

Second week   *Dear diary*

Keeping a diary or journal can sound like a tedious activity, but its effect can be therapeutic as you move your mind's burdens onto paper.

You can be completely original in what you write; no one else will be using the same words in the same way as you. A diary can take any form; it can be just a few jottings of what happened yesterday, or a random collection of thoughts as they enter your mind. It does not have to mean anything, as it is not for anyone else and you don't even have to read it yourself. Just feel the pleasure of capturing your thoughts, forget the grammar, spelling and all the rules, just let the words spill onto the page. Writing is a great way to clear your mind, and get all your concerns out of your head. Your diary becomes a friend that you can confide in or grumble to.

If you have concerns about someone discovering your diary, then simply shred what you have written as soon as you have finished. Then it becomes more like a private conversation with a friend, you wouldn't want to record those conversations would you?

Writing with a pen rather than a keyboard can be very satisfying. In this age of information technology we get few opportunities to use our handwriting.

Daily tasks

Grab a few minutes each day, ideally first thing in the morning before you talk to anyone, read, watch TV or listen to the radio. Get up a few minutes earlier than your usual rise time and spend those few minutes putting pen to paper. Let these be the first raw thoughts that enter your mind. The more time you can spend at this the better. Don't force it. If you have nothing to say, then simply describe where you are and how you feel. The closer you can do this to the point at which you wake up the better. This is a great time, before your mind starts to busy itself with thoughts about the day ahead.

Now PAUSE Reading

After you have completed a week of diary updates.

Resume reading

Personal notes

What worked well for you?

What did you discover?

How did this make you feel?

End of week review

If you have found keeping a journal helpful, then why not make this a part of your daily routine? Or just dip in as the mood takes you.

Workshop – first workshop

Before we begin to learn new calming techniques over the coming weeks, we will visit the supermarket 'workshop' (or your location of choice) to remind ourselves how it feels before we do any more work on calming our mind and emotions.

Now PAUSE Reading

Visit your supermarket for your normal weekly shopping, this time as you walk about be aware how you feel about the whole experience.

Resume reading

Personal notes ✎

How did you feel?

Workshop review

After your supermarket visit, make a few brief notes about anything that happened and record your feelings about the visit. We will come back to this later.

Chapter 2   Distracting your busy mind

The aim of the exercises over the next few weeks is to discover new ways of distracting your mind away from its usual busy chatter. We will come back to this in future weeks as a way of focusing your mind and grounding yourself when things begin to get stressful.

Our culture demands that we are continuously busy and occupied, whilst rest time is considered idle and lazy. One of the consequences of this is that we begin to forget who we are, by becoming so immersed in our busy life, always looking forwards to the next activity in our schedule.

Over the next few weeks we will simply begin to distract the focus of our attention away from the busy stuff in life to more calming thoughts by becoming more aware of our self through our senses. The aim is to snatch a few brief seconds of calm at a time during our daily activities.

We are looking to find one or two techniques that work in distracting your mind away from its chatter. If some exercises do nothing for you after a couple of days, then simply move onto the next until you find a method that works.

How will I know which technique works for me?

This is very personal, with different techniques working for different people. You cannot determine which suits you by reading about it. The only way to discover is by attempting the exercises, during a normal day. When you experience a brief moment of calm, there will be a sensation of stillness in your mind as if you have lost time. When this first happens you tend to be unaware of the stillness of your mind but notice the moment your mind begins to chatter again, as the calm ends and normal incessant thinking resumes.

If you have experienced this once, it can happen again. The more often you practice this, the more you will achieve stillness. We will come back to use your personal technique later in the book as a calm place to go when things become emotionally challenging.

First week   *Reflections*

This week we are going to get to know ourselves better.

We tend to notice all the imperfections in our bodies, all those small blemishes that feel as if they disfigure us. Society praises the impossible perfect body, so most of us then have hang ups about the way that we look, and we begin to avoid seeing our reflection.

So let's take a break from all the social pressure this week and just be a little more compassionate towards our self.

Go and stand in front of a mirror, and marvel at how amazing you are. Don't just think about this, do it right now.

When is the last time you seriously looked at your reflection? For me the last time that I spent any time pondering my own reflection was as a child. I could spend ages pulling funny faces at myself. As you view your refection forget society's ideas of the perfect body and just see yourself as you are. You are totally unique; there is no one else exactly like you. Take a tour around your face, look deeply into your own eyes, and observe all the colours and textures of your skin and hair.

Daily tasks

Over the coming week , every time you glance into a mirror, just pause for a long minute and have a proper look at yourself, move your head around, get to know its shape and pull some funny faces, try out your range of facial expressions – show surprise, smile, frown, and squint. You can take pulling funny faces to the next level. Why not try gurning, which has the side benefit of toning your facial muscles!

Usually we just glance at ourselves in mirrors, to distract our mind we need to get into the habit of just pausing for a few moments. When you are next face to face with your reflection, hold your gaze for a few seconds and look deeply into your own eyes. What do you see?

Say hello to yourself, acknowledge your amazing existence. This sounds so easy yet can be surprisingly challenging.

Look for any opportunity during your day to recognise your refection, in window or shiny surface. Bring your attention to your image for a brief moment and then why not depart with a discrete wink.

Now PAUSE Reading

After a week of becoming aware of your reflection has passed.

Resume reading

Personal notes

What worked well for you?

What did you discover?

How did this make you feel?

Second week   Eating

When did you last notice the flavours and textures of the food that you ate? We tend to treat eating as a way of re-fuelling our bodies; it has become a tedious task to be squeezed in when we have a few minutes free in our busy schedule.

Approached differently eating can be a soothing, relaxing activity and another opportunity to distract our chattering mind. This is not comfort eating, but a focused awareness upon your food.
Fast food encourages fast eating and rush to get on with the next activity in your life, with the result that it just agitates your mind.

Cooking slow food is another approach for slowing your mind, purposefully preparing food slowly and then eating slowly gives your mind a break from the breakneck pace of life. Meal times become a calm oasis in your daily routine.

Daily tasks
If you tend to do other things such as watch television whilst eating, switch it off and just sit quietly and eat. If you are eating with others have a conversation, this has the desirable effect of slowing your eating. Try eating slowly, chewing your food fully before swallowing, notice all the subtle textures and the way in which the flavours change as you chew your food.

Whether it is your breakfast, lunch or dinner, this is a nice time for reflection, so let's consider where the ingredients came from, what plants or animals and where they may have lived. Visualise the whole cycle of life, of the seeds being sown and germinating and the passage of the seasons, the plant's life spent in the sun and rain, growing up against gravity, before being harvested, transported and processed for you. Imagine how many people have worked to bring your meal here. Become aware that your food is so much more than a plate of fuel.

As you eat focus your minds attention upon your tongue, follow its movement around your mouth, the changing flavours, textures and temperatures as you chew your food. Let your mind become occupied with the busy activity of your tongue for as long as you can. You should find that the usual chattering quietens for a while.

Now PAUSE Reading

After a week of being aware of your eating has passed.

Resume reading

Personal notes ✎

What worked well for you?

What did you discover?

How did this make you feel?

Third week   *Listening*

Listening can be used to create stillness in your mind, since it requires that you focus your attention away from the usual chattering. This gives your mind a little light relief.

Right now, just pause for a moment and become aware of all the different sounds around you, the distant sounds and those closer to you. Just zoom in and out on the various sounds. How many different sounds can you hear? Can you identify all the sounds? Can you hear traffic, people, birds, the wind or rain? Note the different qualities of each sound.

Have you noticed how this has occupied your mind completely, distracting it from the usual incessant stream of thinking?

Daily tasks

Grab any opportunities that you can during the coming days to listen to the sounds around you. You can do this anywhere, in the home or office, whilst travelling or shopping. Try to get into the habit of just reflecting for a few moments on the sounds around you. If you get the opportunity to safely close your eyes, you become aware of even more sounds.

Let your mind become totally distracted from its thoughts with the sounds that you can hear. Surf the sounds, travel your acoustic landscape, zoom in and out of specific sounds. It is amazing what is going on about us. Every moment lost in sound is a moment of calm for your mind, and a moment free of stress.

Now PAUSE Reading

Complete a week of listening awareness before you resume reading. However, if you find this task doesn't distract your mind after a couple of days, resume your reading.

Resume reading

Personal notes

What worked well for you?

What did you discover?

How did this make you feel?

Fourth week   *Touching*

Touch is a much underused sense, how often do we truly feel the world around us? We normally move through our environment seeing things but paying little interest to how it feels. Your whole body is continuously sensing its environment but you hardly ever notice.

Begin by noticing the texture of the pages in the book, the clothes on your body your skin and hair. Become familiar with your sense of touch and the sensation of your whole body.

If you can find a quiet undisturbed place, lie down flat on the floor with your head supported and comfortable. If it helps, listen to some calming music. Just take a few slow deep breaths and relax. Now starting with your big toe on your right foot, concentrate all your thoughts on the toe and notice how the skin on your toe feels, perhaps you can feel the fabric of a sock. Once you have felt your big toe, move onto the skin of the toe next to it and repeat the exercise moving to your sole, heel, ankle up to your thigh then repeat for the other leg, your abdomen, each arm your neck and head. After taking a very slow sensory tour around your body's skin, end by noticing the feeling sensation of your whole body; this creates a really calming relaxing sensation.

Daily tasks

As you move about your daily routine, begin to notice the texture of the world about you. When passing a wall feel the texture of the brick or stone, let your hand brush against things as you as you pass. Experience the texture of as many materials as possible during the week ahead.

The moment you touch a surface bring your minds attention to your finger tips, disarming the chatter of your mind for a few moments.

Now PAUSE Reading

Complete a week of touching awareness before you resume reading. However, if you find this task doesn't distract your mind after a couple of days, resume your reading.

Resume reading

Personal notes ✎

What worked well for you?

What did you discover?

How did this make you feel?

Fifth week   *Smell*

We tend to forget how powerful our sense of smell is. How often do you actually notice smells during the day, unless it is something very pungent. If elderly people are re-introduced to a smell from their earliest childhood, it can invoke flashback memories back to that time, memories which they can't remember having. The more you focus your awareness upon your sense of smell, the more sensitive it seems to become and you will begin to notice an emerging rich landscape of smells.

Why not take a few sniffs now. What can you smell? Try to work out where the scents are coming from. A plant, the material from your sofa…..

Daily tasks

When you are entering or leaving a building or room, just take a moment to sniff the air what does this tell you. It can be good fun to re-discover a world you may not have noticed since your childhood.

Now PAUSE Reading

Complete a week of olfactory awareness before you resume reading. However, if you find this task doesn't distract your mind after a couple of days, resume your reading.

Resume reading

Personal notes 🖎

What worked well for you?

What did you discover?

How did this make you feel?

Sixth week   Lists revisited

This is a small twist to the use of list making that we started back in week one which helped to unburden your mind, and reduce the churning thoughts which are repeating, all the things that you feel you must remember to do. However, when it comes down to it, many of the items that you have listed on the long, low-priority list really don't matter that much to you, otherwise you would have done them.

In six months to a year's time, your long list will remain mostly unchanged with all those items still there. That being the case, let's just delete the low priority list. Every time that you bring out your to-do lists they are putting you under pressure, by reminding you of all those things that you feel you must do. Your mind can play tricks, trying to keep you busy all the time with thoughts of 'I can't be idle, I really should be doing something else from my big list'. If we now remove the long list, ideally by destroying it, then you can free yourself up from unnecessary pressures that you have put upon yourself.

Destroy the long, low-priority list by ceremoniously shredding and re-cycling it. You won't miss it, if there is something important on the list then it will pop up again and you will put it on your short urgent list. This is just another way to release self imposed pressures and to lighten your mind. It is a liberating feeling destroying all those nagging tasks that you feel that you should be doing, but in reality are not that important.

Daily tasks

This week we will re-evaluate your short priority list; do you really need to do all those things immediately. Be careful not to start putting items that were on your less urgent long list onto the short urgent list. Be ruthless and only record tasks that need completing over the coming days.

Now PAUSE Reading

Complete a week of keeping only the most urgent of tasks on the short priority list before you resume reading.

Resume reading

Personal notes

What worked well for you?

What did you discover?

How did this make you feel?

Workshop – distracting your busy mind

Summary

Over the past few weeks we have been trying various ways to distract our mind from its busy thoughts. Hopefully you will have found one or more techniques that allow you to snatch the occasional few seconds of calm during your daily activities. You will have experienced moments when your mind was still, free of its usual chatter. This is very personal, with different techniques working for different people.

Workshop activity

The supermarket is an excellent place to challenge you emotionally, few of us enjoy our shopping trips there, so it makes an excellent place to try out some of the mind calming techniques that you are learning. During your next visit to the supermarket (or your workshop location of choice) we are going to practice all the various techniques from this chapter. But first glance back over the previous weeks to remind yourself of the different techniques that you have explored.

Perform your shopping in the usual way and pay attention to the following:

Reflections Become aware of reflections of your face in the glass and metalwork.

Eating Take the opportunity to eat slowly in the Café, become more aware of the food you are eating.

Listening	Be aware of the sounds within the building, the hum of machines, people talking and the clatter of trolleys.
Touching	Note the texture of fruit, vegetables and the various types of packaging. Feel the changes in temperature.
Smell	The differences in smell from one aisle to the next can be quite marked. Note the smells of the fruit and vegetables.

Now PAUSE Reading

Visit your supermarket for your normal weekly shopping, this time being more aware of the experience then resume reading.

Resume reading

Personal notes ✏

What worked well for you?

What did you discover?

How did this make you feel?

Workshop review

Hopefully this will have distracted your mind from its usual chatter and created a much calmer shopping experience than usual. Just note how simple it is to calm your mind – if only you can remember to do it. This just comes with practice, I now find myself enjoying trips to the supermarket, after previously being irritated.

What can you take from this chapter?

If you have found a couple of techniques that allow you to distract your mind for brief moments, then consider using them daily from now on. The more you access your calm, the easier it will come. We will then be able to build on this later in the book to serve as a life raft for you when things become really tough emotionally. With this calm come lots of other benefits such as increased energy.

Chapter 3 Further distraction techniques

In the previous chapter we used our senses as a way to distract our busy mind. In this chapter we shall use the world which surrounds us to discover more distractions. We will revisit these techniques in future weeks as a way of focusing your mind when things begin to get emotionally uncomfortable.

Over the next few weeks we will simply begin to distract the focus of our mind's attention away from the busy stuff of life to more calming thoughts by becoming more aware of the world in which we live.

Our aim is to find one or two techniques that work for you in distracting your mind away from its chatter. If some exercises do nothing for you after a couple of days, then simply move onto the next until you find a method that works.

First week   Walking

If you have periods of walking during your normal working day, then this is a great opportunity for distracting your mind. Walking is a rhythmic action and lends itself to stilling the mind.

When you are walking you are normally going between doing things, so walking is an opportunity to rest your mind between periods of activity. So let your body do the work and give your mind a rest when you are walking this week.

Try to avoid doing other activities whilst you walk over the coming week, such as talking on the phone or listening to music. Simply bring your minds attention to your walking.

Daily tasks

Please practice these exercises only where it is safe to do so, since you will be attempting to distract your mind slightly.
There is a walking relaxation technique called Peripatetic meditation which is great for distracting the mind. Whenever you have a few minutes of walking, it is an easy exercise to perform.

This works best when walking on the flat, so you're walking rhythm remains the same. Walk briskly but not so quickly that you are out of breath; there is no need to exert yourself. This should be enjoyable and comfortable. As you walk become aware of your foot falls and the feeling of the pressure of your body weight on each foot. At the same time, count from one to ten with each step. After a while you mind will begin to calm.

The act of counting whilst walking tends to block out some of the mind chatter and prevents your mind 'mulling' over distracting thoughts.

If you are a fast walker always rushing about, try slowing your walking speed down to a snail's pace. Walk at the speed of a child, this can be very difficult at first, but forces you to become more aware of the world about you.

Now *PAUSE* Reading

If it is appropriate for you, complete a week of walking awareness before you resume reading. However, if you find this task doesn't distract your mind after several attempts, resume your reading.

Resume reading

Personal notes ✎

What worked well for you?

What did you discover?

How did this make you feel?

Second week   *Look up*

The next time you are outside, observe how many people walk with their heads down, in quiet contemplation of the pavement. When was the last time that you noticed the sky, the clouds, these huge magnificent mountains of water vapour tend to go unnoticed. If you walk with your head looking up the other surprising thing that you notice is the architecture of the buildings. In our towns we are surrounded by high ornate stone work that few people ever notice. The act of lifting your eyes whilst you walk also tends to lift your spirits away from the mundane.

Notice the horizon, where your world meets the sky; slowly travel along your horizon from one side to the other. What can you see? Become familiar with your place in the wider world, beyond the microcosm of daily life. See the broader picture which is wider than your life and recognise and feel your part within it.

Daily tasks

As you walk about get into the habit of glancing upwards more often, look up at the roofs and buildings it can be surprising what you see. A bonus of glancing upwards as you walk is that it tends to straighten your back and improve your posture. This in turn allows your body to breathe more freely.

A fun technique to try is 'wide angle vision' this involves looking directly ahead and relaxing your focus slightly so that your vision becomes wider allowing you to see everything from your sides down to your feet. If it is safe to do so, try this when walking

49

down the street, it is like having 'super hero' vision and you become aware of everything happening around you.

Now PAUSE Reading

Complete a week of looking upwards before you resume reading. However, if you find this task doesn't distract your mind after a couple of days, resume your reading.

Resume reading

Personal notes 🖊

What worked well for you?

What did you discover?

How did this make you feel?

Third week *Weather*

The weather is always about us and shapes our lives in so many ways; this makes it a convenient distraction. The added advantage of the weather is the way that it changes seasonally through small daily changes. For many of us in more temperate climes our weather can change quite dramatically from day to day, but we rarely notice until it inconveniences us in some way.

Daily tasks

As you step outside just take note of the colour of the sky. Notice the changing shapes and textures of the clouds, let your mind wander with the clouds for a moment or two. Feel the wind on your face, as it follows the contours and shape of your profile. What is the temperature of the air? If it is raining, how does the rain feel upon your skin? Experience the feel of the weather; let it distract your mind. The infinite variety of changes the weather brings makes it an excellent distraction, because there is usually something different to yesterday. Get into the habit of glancing out of windows at the sky, register the changes since you last looked.

Now PAUSE Reading

Complete a week of being aware of the weather before you resume reading. However, if you find this task doesn't distract your mind after a couple of days, resume your reading.

Resume reading

Personal notes ✎

What worked well for you?

What did you discover?

How did this make you feel?

Fourth week   Water

Water is wonderful stuff, kids and animals love it, it has amazing properties and science still does not fully understand it. It feels great on your skin; it can be refreshing or relaxing. We like to bathe in it and drink it. The Earth's surface is mostly water, appearing blue from space, evolutionary theory even suggests that we originally came from the seas. Water accounts for almost half our body weight, so any water that we drink will become a small part of us and the quality of the water will affect your constitution. Try tasting various sources of water, bottled mineral waters etc. If your sense of taste is well developed, you can taste big differences between them. Be aware that if you predominantly drink beverages that have strong or sweet flavours then your sense of taste will have become desensitised and it may take time to get used to drinking water again. But it does provide additional health benefits.

Drink some water and reflect upon the thought that the one thing we cannot survive without is water, the giver of life. A slight shift in your thinking can have another calming effect upon your life. Reflect upon this and the long journey the water has taken whenever you drink.

Daily tasks

Try to drink water more often during the week ahead, notice the different tastes and reflect upon where it has come from and that it is soon to be part of you.

If you take a shower, experience the water upon your body and its refreshing energising affect. It you take a bath, notice the relaxing sensation of the water upon your skin.

Every time you come into contact with water, just notice it for what it is. Many of the world's ancient cultures held water in great regard. It still holds many mysteries for us today.

Now PAUSE Reading

Complete a week of being aware of water before you resume reading. However, if you find this task doesn't distract your mind after a couple of days, resume your reading.

Resume reading

Personal notes

What worked well for you?

What did you discover?

How did this make you feel?

Fifth week   *Conscious Breathing*

Many of our ancient cultures place an emphasis upon breath work, and its importance in helping prevent illness and speed our recovery from sickness. It has been observed that we change which nostril we breathe through at different times of the day, the left nostril is used when relaxed and the right when active. During the night the nostril used changes our body temperature. Left for cool and right for warm. The side on which you sleep will influence which nostril is used. If you are uncomfortable try sleeping on your other side to change your temperature.

Breathing is a great form of relaxation and is meditative; it distracts your busy mind away from its incessant ramblings and allows it to focus on your breath.

Breathing connects you to your environment, with each breath you are drawing in air that has been touched by countless people, plants and animals, so your environment becomes a part of you. You are not as separate and as individual as you may at first think.

Just take a moment, close your mouth and observe which nostril you are breathing through.

Slowly breathe out through your mouth completely pushing the air out with your diaphragm, so that any old stale air in your lungs is pushed out.
Relax and rest your tongue on the top of your mouth and breathe in through your nose, just let the air flood into your lungs. Repeat this several times, slowly following your breath in and out.

Daily tasks

Occasionally take a moment during the day to breathe consciously, follow the air in through your nose, feel its progress down through your nose down the back of your throat and feel it expand your lungs. Push out your stomach as your lungs fill. When your lungs are full, hold your breath for a few seconds before allowing the stale air to rush out. Follow the progress of your breath back out through your mouth. As you keep your minds awareness upon your breath, your minds chatter begins to fade away into the background.

Become aware of your breathing, this simple movement helps keep you alive, yet we seldom notice unless we are out of breath after exerting ourselves.

Reflect upon your integration with the environment, as you breathe in some of the air will become a part of your body and as you breathe out a small part of your body will become part of the plants and trees around you.

Now PAUSE Reading

Complete a week of breathing awareness before you resume reading. However, if you find this task doesn't distract your mind after a couple of days, resume your reading.

Resume reading

Personal notes ✎

What worked well for you?

What did you discover?

How did this make you feel?

Sixth week   *In nature*

Nature is the ideal antidote for a stressed mind and turbulent emotions, what's more it is free. Forget your expensive drugs, simply spend more time in natural spaces.

We have evolved for outside living and yet the average North American now spends more than 80% of their life indoors. Natural spaces provide the habitat that our minds have evolved over tens of thousands of years to experience, so by spending time in such spaces we are giving our minds a natural break.

This week we will be taking advantage of Mother nature who provides a wonderful place for creating a still mind. The natural world can be gentle on all your senses. Simply increasing your exposure to nature with daily walks in local green spaces can make a huge difference to the state of your mind and your happiness.

Daily tasks

Attempt to spend some time each day in a natural space such as a garden, park or by some trees. Sit and relax for a few moments and allow the natural life about you to infuse your body. Share your breath with the plants and trees around you and immerse yourself in the plant and bird life. Take a deep breath, relax and let it all flow over you, now how does that feel. Become re-connected to nature, beginning with your feet, feel the ground under you. Observe the detail of the shape and texture of the plants and trees around you.

Let your attention fall upon a flower or leaf, see it and be aware of it but don't think about it by labelling it with names. Hear the rustle of leaves in the wind, and the hum of insects flying by. Immerse yourself and your senses in the natural activity around you, and then become aware of the stillness of the plants and trees. Let this stillness envelop your mind.

Don't use the weather as an excuse not to go out, all forms of weather bring something different to observe and experience.

Work time lunch break's are an excellent opportunity for getting out, if you usually sit in front of your computer to eat lunch, break routine this week and go for a walk in a green space.

Now PAUSE Reading

Complete a week of being aware of nature before you resume reading. However, if you find this task doesn't distract your mind after a couple of days, resume your reading.

Resume reading

Personal notes 🖊

What worked well for you?

What did you discover?

How did this make you feel?

Seventh week   Celestial awareness

Observe the procession of the Sun and moon across the sky and how their paths change with the different seasons. If you ignore the occasional aircraft trails, your sky appears almost the same as it did for our primitive ancestors thousands of years ago.
Also reflect upon the Sun during the hours of darkness, rather than above you it is now under you on the other side of the Earth.

When you next see the Sun, remember that the Earth was created from the Sun. Hence your bodies very essence is from the Sun.

If you get the chance on a clear night to be away from streetlights, go outside and look up. Observe all the stars, planets and the moon; reflect upon how grand it all is. If you are lucky you may even see shooting stars. Widen your awareness beyond your immediate surroundings to our planet Earth, the stars and space.

Daily tasks

Feel the Sun's light upon your skin and the sensation as it penetrates your flesh and warms you within. Slowly breathe in the warmth of the Sun into your lungs, drink its warmth and light.

Try to witness the Sun rise or Sun set each day and note the procession of the Sun across the sky, if it is cloudy try to imagine where the sun is.

Now PAUSE Reading

Complete a week of being aware of the bigger picture before you resume reading. However, if you find this task doesn't distract your mind after a couple of days, resume your reading.

Resume reading

Personal notes

What worked well for you?

What did you discover?

How did this make you feel?

Eighth week   Experience your world

Become aware of how you react to the world around you, not emotionally but physically. Over the past few weeks you have become more aware of your individual senses, you can now start to pull all this together and take in the complete sensation of sight, sound, touch, taste and hearing. Try to experience it all as a child, without giving things names, just experience all your senses at once. For example with your sight, see it all, when is the last time that you watched a shadow? Many artists still have the ability to see as a child and experience everything for the first time, when painting they will see all the minute details in a scene. During your busy life you experience the world as a stream of snapshot images; we rarely take the time to view the whole scene. Try to take this approach with all your senses, not just your sight. Experience the feel, smell, sound and sight of the world about you as if for the first time.

Daily tasks

A great way to reduce stress is to calm your chattering mind by bringing your attention to the whole of your environment about you. Using all your senses at once. This is like listening to the music played by an orchestra, rather than all the individual instruments. Just grab moments during the day – any time at all and just expand your awareness to take in the whole symphony of your senses from the world around you. Just contemplate it, letting it wash over you. Try not to focus on any individual smell/taste/sound/sight/feeling but just let the whole lot play over you. A few brief seconds can be enough to allow you to feel your whole body's senses as one.

Now PAUSE Reading

Complete a week of being aware of the world about you through all your senses before you resume reading. However, if you find this task doesn't distract your mind after a couple of days, resume your reading.

Resume reading

Personal notes

What worked well for you?

What did you discover?

How did this make you feel?

Workshop – further distraction techniques

Summary

Over the past few weeks we have been trying various ways to distract our mind form its busy thoughts, by using the world about you. Hopefully you will have found one or more techniques that allow you to snatch a brief few seconds of calm during your daily activities.

Workshop activity

During your next visit to the supermarket we are going to practice some of techniques from the past two chapters. But first glance back over the previous weeks to remind yourself of the different techniques that you have explored.   This chapter is a little tricky because many of the activities are based outside, but it does make it more fun.

Perform your shopping in the usual way and pay attention to the following:

Walking	Become aware of your foot falls. If you are dashing about try slowing your pace.
Look up	Lift your eyes from the shelves and see what the store looks like up above you.
Weather	Can you feel the changes in temperature as you move about? Is there a light breeze from the air conditioning?
Water	Take a drink of water, reflect upon its source.
Breathing	Focus upon your breath flowing in and out.
In Nature	Note the texture and shapes of fruit and vegetables.

Big picture   No Sun visible in here, so note the intensity of the lighting.

Experience   Whilst you are waiting in the checkout queue, just pause for a moment and feel the whole experience of the store.

Also apply those techniques that you found helpful during chapter two.

Now PAUSE Reading

Visit your supermarket for your normal weekly shopping, this time being more aware of the experience then resume reading.

Resume reading

Personal notes ✐

What worked well for you?

What did you discover?

How did this make you feel?

Workshop review

Hopefully during this visit to the supermarket you will have succeeded in distracting your mind from its usual chatter, creating a much calmer shopping experience than usual. Just note how simple it is to calm your mind.

What can you take from this chapter?

If you have found a couple of techniques that allow you to distract your mind for brief moments, then consider using them daily from now on. The more you access your calm, the easier it will come. We will then be able to build on this later in the book to serve as a life raft for you when things become tough emotionally.

Chapter 4   Rest your mind

Approached the correct way, idleness and day-dreaming can provide excellent opportunities for a resting your mind.

Let us just pause and reflect for a moment on what we are trying to achieve. The reason for practising the exercises in this book is to free your mind from the emotional chatter and over activity that occupies our day. We only use a small percentage of our brain power for conscious thinking, the rest of your brain is busy running your body, breathing, digesting your last meal and innumerable other activities. It does not happen all of its own accord but through the careful organisation of all your bodily systems. Just think how difficult it was to ride a bike for the first time, how tricky it was to simultaneously balance, turn the pedals and steer. Once you have undergone the difficulty of learning how to control the bike, your subconscious mind does it all automatically for you.

When you are sick, it is not the doctors and the medicine that heal your body, but your own body. The doctors can help, but at the end of the day it is your brain that is busy orchestrating all the resources that you have to fight off the illness. You can observe this whenever a cut heals itself, without you having to think how. So if we can accept that your brain plays a major part in maintaining your health, then we can infer that if your brain is not functioning 100% then your body's health may be impaired too.

Taking this idea a little further, if you can provide regular opportunities to rest your brain a little with some mind relaxation then there will be a direct benefit to your health. This is all very slow and gentle, but if you can calm your mind you will find that your health will slowly improve with it. The only problem is that it can take a lot longer to recover than the time that you have subjected yourself to all the stresses.

First week   Embrace idleness

From the moment we wake we are working hard at keeping our mind entertained and occupied in an effort not to become bored. If we assume for now that being idle can have the effect of resting the mind, then this opens new opportunities because idleness tends to lead to day dreaming which is like a mini break for your mind.

Just pause for a few minutes and do nothing, let any background noises just wash over you, rest your focus on this book and look through it, as if you were focusing on the floor a few metres away....... How long is it before you become uncomfortable and are itching to do something, or your mind drifts off with busy thoughts again?

Daily tasks

Look for opportunities during the day to become idle, it only needs to be a few minutes here or there. Simply sit and do nothing. Switch off, relax and chill out, remember how it feels to be idle, embrace it.

Other opportunities for idleness present themselves whilst waiting for things, whether it is for the kettle to boil or standing in a queue. If you are queuing you become fixated on the slow people in front of you. This week try ignoring your progress in queues and become aware of your feet on the floor and the sounds about you. Look around at the people and feel your place in the building. Before you know it, your wait will be over, and you will be so much calmer.

Now PAUSE Reading

Complete a week of idle moments before you resume reading.

Resume reading

Personal notes ✎

What worked well for you?

What did you discover?

How did this make you feel?

Second week   *Travelling*

This week we continue with the same theme as last week, but we focus upon commuting and travelling. If you have a regular daily commute then this exercise is the one for you. Obviously if you are the driver then you need to show some restraint when it comes to relaxation.

Daily tasks

If you spend a lot of your travel time reading or listening to a personal music player to occupy your time then this could be quite a challenge. Put your reading material or music player to one side and just be relaxed and take in the world around you, observe your fellow commuters and the views outside as they slide past your window. Just feel what it is like to spend some time in mindless contemplation or idleness, if your mind begins to chatter away, acknowledge the thoughts and let them drift away. Let your mind be free for a while, to roam about with its own thoughts.

Now PAUSE Reading

Complete a week of practising being idle whilst travelling before you resume reading.

Resume reading

Personal notes

What worked well for you?

What did you discover?

How did this make you feel?

Third week   Clock watching

We live our lives in a very ordered way using clocks and calendars to structure our days. This can give the feeling of being trapped or restrained by time. It becomes our master and provokes impatience and frustration. We never seem to have enough time to do all those things that we need to do. So clocks add to the stress in our lives.

It is difficult to operate in our modern world without knowing what the time is, we still need to catch a bus or arrive at work at the correct time. But we can reduce the impact of time on our lives by not referring to it so much.

Daily tasks

If you find yourself awake during the night and would normally check the time this can give rise to the frustration of: I have only slept for an hour, or I have been awake for ages. By turning the clock away and not reading the time, you can lessen these frustrations. Just turn over and ignore what the time is. This removes the pressure that time creates when you are having disturbed sleep.

During the daytime, try not wearing a watch and avoid referring to the time on your mobile phone. You will be surprised how many clocks there are in the world around you, I tend to glance at other peoples watches to get the current time if I really need it. Or you could ask, getting involved with those around you as an added benefit.

Now PAUSE Reading

Complete a week of using clocks less before you resume reading.

Resume reading

Personal notes ✎

What worked well for you?

What did you discover?

How did this make you feel?

End of week review

This very subtly just loosens your connection to the time and gives you a little freedom; you start to feel less constrained.

When you know the time exactly you tend to squeeze as much as you can out of the time available. You become pressurised by the time available and any delay becomes stressful.

Having only a vague idea about time encourages you to set off early, so your journey takes longer. The positive outcome can be that you are more relaxed because any delays become less of a problem with your loose schedule. There is also the benefit that now that you have more slack in your schedule, there are opportunities for a little idleness.

Fourth week   *Less busy*

I sometimes wonder if we have developed a new greeting, that is beginning to take over from 'hello, how are you', that is 'hello what have you been doing'. We are always expected to be doing 'something' that has some interest to other people. If we take a week's vacation, everyone wants to know where we have been and what we were doing. Even weekends can be a challenge with people asking what you have done.

We are under continuous social pressure to be active all the time. Our challenge this week is to adopt a different approach. Don't plan to do things all the time, just potter about, do stuff that has no interest to others but what takes your interest. It may not be headline grabbing, but if it helps you relax a little then it has to be a precious use of your valuable time. Oh yes and the added bonus is that it tends to be a lot less costly.

Just offload another of the little pressures that society burdens you with.

Daily tasks

Become aware of people telling you how busy they are or how often you are asked about your activity. Play a game and start answering with 'Oh I just chilled out this weekend'. This tends to throw people, but after a time you will find them questioning why they are so busy.

Now PAUSE Reading

Complete a week of being less busy before you resume reading.

Resume reading

Personal notes

What worked well for you?

What did you discover?

How did this make you feel?

Fifth week   *Soothing music*

We have now spent several weeks reducing the chatter of our mind; it's now time for some gentle relaxation. Relaxation can be very difficult, typically the only time we are relaxing fully is when we sleep. Finding the time to relax can be a challenge, there are always lots of other things that we could be doing, such as items on our to-do list. We become skilled at inventing reasons why we have no time to relax. Against all this is the awful thought of doing nothing. Sitting in silence can be really difficult, so listening to music without words can be a gentle way of occupying the mind for a while.

Let's have a go now, find some soothing music without words or a distracting melody. If you do not have anything suitable, then plan to obtain some music early in the week.

Close your eyes and let your mind wander with the music. If you can, try visualizing a world of your own and let the music take you on a journey through your imagined world. If, like me, you struggle with visualization, let the music simply create a 'feeling'. As the music progresses and changes allow it to change the world that you are experiencing. Let the music paint a picture for you and slowly take you through the picture, travel about under the direction of the music.

Now, when I say listen, I mean really listen. Just sitting there and becoming totally immersed in the music.

We usually do other things whilst listening to music, reading, travelling, cooking, working etc. The music becomes of secondary importance pushed into the background.

Daily tasks

This week try to find some quiet time alone, if you have them use some headphones. Select some music that you can really lose yourself in, something atmospheric perhaps instrumental. Whatever works for you. Get comfortable relax, close your eyes and travel with the music, move your attention around the various instruments. As soon as you find your mind chattering, acknowledge the thought and then bring your attention back to the music.

We under use our hearing, it can take a few sessions to really get back into using our hearing fully, its like watching a film in 3D compared to a black and white TV. When we bring our full attention to the music, it can be quite an amazing experience.

Now PAUSE Reading

Complete a week of relaxing to music before you resume reading.

Resume reading

Personal notes

What worked well for you?

What did you discover?

How did this make you feel?

Sixth week   Day dreaming

Day dreaming is an opportunity to rest your mind during the day and give it a chance to play. If you can get into the day dreaming state, your mind tends to suspend its incessant chatter. As a child it seemed much easier to day dream, the mind was less occupied then.

Just have a go now, rest your tongue on the roof of your mouth and breathe in and out slowly and deeply. Become aware of yourself and hold a relaxed gaze on the floor a few metres ahead of you, relax the muscles around the eyes. Take your mind back to an experience that was really enjoyable for you, then let your mind drift. Remain like this for as long as you can without making any effort to day dream. If nothing happens then just treat it as a rest and have a go another day at a different time that may suit you better.

Daily tasks

Repeat the exercise daily at different times until you can find a time and place that suits you best. Bus and train journeys are ideal for you to let your mind float off. You will soon begin to learn what works best for you.

If there are many distractions you may find it easier to daydream with some relaxing background instrumental music.

Idly watch the clouds, observe, let your imagination roam free, can you see faces or animals in the clouds? You can do the same thing when looking into an open fire, or the bark on the trunk of a tree. It is tricky at first because all you see are the clouds, your mind puts a name to them and almost tells you to move on. You can defeat your logical thinking mind by continuing to look at the same view, just soak it up, almost becoming bored so your mind starts to drift off.

Now PAUSE Reading

Complete a week of day dreaming before you resume reading.

Resume reading

Personal notes

What worked well for you?

What did you discover?

How did this make you feel?

End of week review

It can take a while to re-discover day dreaming, but once you find it, you will remember the feeling and be able to re-create it again at will.

Seventh week   *Restful sleep*

Sleep plays a big part in our lives and good quality sleep helps us maintain our calm during our waking hours. If you can enter your sleep in a positive state of mind, it can set the theme for the night's sleeping and dreaming. This can in turn improve the quality of your sleep.

If you have sleep problems, and experience difficulty getting back to sleep once awake, just remember that you cannot force yourself to sleep, it will only happen when your mind is distracted from thinking. So rather than getting up and keeping occupied, just stay relaxed and be satisfied with the thought that you are getting some much needed rest, relaxing and resting your body. Even if you are awake for hours, your body is getting some rest.

If your mind is busy and active, the knack is to distract your mind. Now, different things work for different people but simple techniques such as slowly following your breath in and out, feeling its progress into your nose and down into your lungs can distract your mind for long enough that you eventually fall asleep. Remember, whatever you do, don't occupy your mind with 'thinking' about going to sleep. Try one of the earlier exercises such as an awareness of the sensations of your body.

If you are still struggling to get to sleep, there is a simple trick you can play on your mind to bring about sleep. Relax, close your eyes and gently try to stay awake for another two hours. By concentrating upon staying awake, this usually has the opposite effect and you will fall asleep faster than usual.

Daily tasks

At the end of the day as you settle down to go to sleep; just take a moment to reflect on a few of the good things that happened during the day. No matter how insignificant they may be. For example, things you saw or heard. Then briefly think how you would like things to go positively the next day. Keep it simple do not get into thoughts about how you are going to organise the next day, just what you would like the outcomes to be. Keep it short and simple. Doing this routinely every night can have a positive effect upon your outlook, and create a calm mood for your sleep.

The moment you wake in the morning, just capture the feeling that your last dream left with you. Don't worry about the detail of the dream, but if you are lucky enough to remember your dreams then why not try making some quick notes. The interpretation of dreams can be fun. But remember that they mean different things to every individual. What you can rely upon is the feeling that the dream left you with. Just reflect upon the feeling, don't worry about analysing the detail of your dream.

Now *PAUSE* Reading

Complete a week of structured sleep before you resume reading.

Resume reading

Personal notes ✎

What worked well for you?

What did you discover?

How did this make you feel?

Workshop – rest your mind

Summary

Over the past few weeks we have been trying various ways to rest our mind. Hopefully you will have found one or more techniques that allow you to find some opportunities to slow down and give your mind a break.

Workshop activity

During your next visit to the supermarket (or your workshop of choice) we are going to practice some of the techniques from this chapter. But first glance back over the previous weeks to remind yourself of the different methods that you have explored.

Allow a little more time for your shopping trip. Perform your shopping in the usual way and pay attention to the following:

Idleness   Be deliberately idle for a couple of minutes, try browsing magazines or books.

Travelling   On your way to and from the supermarket, take a break from the radio/music/reading. Let your mind drift a little.

Clocks   Try not to clock watch during your visit.

Less busy   Stop, take a break and have a coffee at the café.

Day dream   Whilst taking your coffee, stare into space and daydream for a couple of minutes.

Also apply those techniques that you found helpful during earlier chapters.

Now PAUSE Reading

Visit your supermarket for your normal weekly shopping, this time set off earlier and allow more time for your shopping. Find opportunities to rest during your shopping. Then resume reading.

Resume reading

Personal notes

What worked well for you?

What did you discover?

How did this make you feel?

Workshop review

Hopefully this has slowed down your shopping visit and created a much calmer experience than usual. Note how simple it is to become calmer, you just need to remember to slow down and give your mind a break.

What can you take from this chapter?

If you have found a couple of techniques that slow you down and give your mind a break, then consider using them daily from now on. The more you drink from your reservoir of calm, the easier it will flow. Also be aware that by slowing down and becoming calmer, your jobs only take a little longer to complete. Is it worth the trade off to you?

Chapter 5   Emotional awareness

We have now established a relationship between ourselves and the world around us, the next step is to become familiar with the way our emotions ebb and flow during the day.

When you release your mind from the continuous burden of work and give it a rest, it tends to fill its time with its own thoughts. For the next few weeks, we become more aware of our thoughts and emotions. This in turn has a gentle calming effect.

First week   *Power listening*

This week we take the listening exercise we did earlier to a new level.

During conversations it is surprising how little we listen and there is this overriding desire of people to have the last word. It is a form of verbal jousting; some people are more inclined than others, they feel that they need to take advantage during a conversation. When you start to listen to your conversations, you become aware that you pay very little attention to the words said by the other person. We are in such a rush to speak after they have spoken, that our mind is busy formulating our next words whilst they are speaking, so we only hear a few of their words.

Daily tasks

When you are holding a conversation, really listen to what the other person is saying; hold back when you feel the temptation to fill a silent gap. Just notice how the other person fills silent gaps. Try to avoid getting the last word in, the temptation to duel.

Become aware of how other people relate to you, don't analyse or try to understand it, just get a feel for the rhythms and style of their conversations when compared to other people that you know. Note the differences between the people who make you feel good after a conversation and those that make you feel drained, as if they have taken some energy from you.

- o Note when you interrupt someone else's speech
- o Notice when you give advice
- o Take your time before speaking
- o Actually listen to what others say.

Now PAUSE Reading

Complete a week of power listening before you resume reading.

Resume reading

Personal notes

What worked well for you?

What did you discover?

How did this make you feel?

Second week   *Emotional changes*

Become aware of how you feel and react to situations as they happen, this is almost like watching and observing yourself acting in a film. If you have a strong emotional response to someone or something, don't worry about why, just let it happen and take note. Observe yourself at the time and then later when everything has calmed down, reflect upon what has happened but resist the temptation to try to explain or understand why.

Daily tasks

During the week ahead observe your emotions and how they ebb and flow throughout the day, you will find that you react differently to various people. Who gives you positive feelings and who leaves unpleasant feelings? How were you feeling before and after? Just simply observe, don't try to get into a complicated analysis of why your emotions are changing and attempting to explain them.

The simple act of observing your emotions can have the gentle effect of creating stillness in your mind.

Now PAUSE Reading

Complete a week of observing your changing emotions before you resume reading.

Resume reading

Personal notes 🖊

What worked well for you?

What did you discover?

How did this make you feel?

Third week   *Repeated thoughts*

Now that you are more aware of the chatter of your mind, just reflect upon the thoughts that keep recurring. Some thoughts will just not go away. Don't try to stop them, but just note that you have seen this one before. Over time this can reduce the frequency of these repeating thoughts.

Daily tasks

Repeat whatever exercise works best for you from earlier in the book, which allows your mind to become idle. Just listen to the thoughts that keep on re-occurring. Pay special attention to those of a negative nature, don't be concerned about the nature of the thoughts, and just acknowledge that they are happening.

Now PAUSE Reading

Complete a week of observing your repeating thoughts before you resume reading.

Resume reading

Personal notes ✎

What worked well for you?

What did you discover?

How did this make you feel?

Fourth week   *Past and future*

Many of our thoughts are worries about the past or future. They keep invading our mind, causing repetitive stress, with little benefit to us. By becoming more aware of these particular thoughts and observing them, you can slowly help to lessen the stress that they cause. This is very easy to say, more challenging to do. But an awareness of what is happening can help reduce their effect upon you.

Disturbing memories from past experiences that keep bubbling back up to the surface of your mind can cause pain in the present, but you cannot change the past by worrying about deeds done. You were different then to how you are now, so you behaved in a way that was appropriate to your life then. You are just keeping memories alive with these recurring thoughts and maintaining pain in the present. All the strain upon your mind about past events and emotions provides no benefit to you today.

In a similar way to past memories, worries about what may or may not happen in your future life, can have a similar impact upon your life. The future has not happened so worrying about it does not change your future; it just adds stress to your present.

Find a quiet place where you will be undisturbed for a few minutes. Relax, close your eyes and listen to the chatter of your mind. Don't worry about what is being said, or listen too closely. Just let your thoughts pass by and listen to the worrying thoughts that come from past experiences or are concerns about future events. Try not to pass judgement on the thoughts just acknowledge them. How many of the thoughts concern the present moment? I suspect none of them. Your mind tends to keep itself occupied with thoughts that are not relevant to this present moment in time.

When you recognise a worrying past or future thought just acknowledge it and let it go, come to see these thoughts as annoying old friends who keep on coming back to you, try greeting them with a wry smile.

Daily tasks

As thoughts flash through your mind each day, just become aware of those thoughts about the past or future, and make a mental note of them. If you are keeping a journal record those thoughts that you have. What is the common theme, is it the same theme from the past or future? As you become aware of these thoughts and acknowledge them, their impact upon you will weaken.

Now PAUSE Reading

Complete a week of observing past and future worries before you resume reading.

Resume reading

Personal notes ✎

What worked well for you?

What did you discover?

How did this make you feel?

Workshop – emotional awareness

Summary

Over the past few weeks we have become more aware of our thoughts and emotions, this awareness can have a gentle calming effect upon those thoughts.

Workshop activity

During your next visit to the supermarket (or your workshop of choice) we are going to practice some of the techniques from this chapter. But first glance back over the previous weeks to remind yourself of the different approaches that you have explored.

Allow more time for your visit and then perform your shopping in the usual way. Apply all those techniques that you found helpful from previous chapters.

Distract your mind from its chatter by becoming more aware of the world around you.

Rest your mind by providing opportunities to slow down and force idle breaks into your schedule. This allows you to become more aware of your emotions.

This time pay special attention to the following:

Listening	When you talk to staff or other customers, become mindful that you are listening carefully.
Emotions	During your visit observe how your emotions change.
Repetition	Note those thoughts that keep repeating.

Past & future Take note of thoughts about past events or worries about things to come.

Now PAUSE Reading

Visit your supermarket for your normal weekly shopping, this time set off earlier and allow more time for your shopping. Observe your changing emotions and thoughts. Then resume reading.

Resume reading

Personal notes ✎

What worked well for you?

What did you discover?

How did this make you feel?

Workshop review

Now you have slowed down your busy mind, you have created opportunities to observe your thoughts and emotions in an impartial way as they arise. Even in the busy environment of the supermarket.

What can you take from this chapter?

All the ground work from the earlier chapters provides you with the space to observe your changing thoughts and emotions. The more you observe your thoughts and emotions impartially; the more they will begin to dissolve away. This is a very slow gentle process but more calm will enter your life.

Chapter 6   Calming your emotions

We are now more aware of our emotions and how they develop during the day. This awareness has the gentle effect of softening the activity of our mind. For the next few weeks we will begin to learn some simple techniques to take this a little further and gently control some of our unwanted emotions.

First week   *When the going gets tough*

If you find yourself in a situation where your emotions are beginning to run out of control, and you are struggling to keep your cool. There is a simple technique that you can use in any situation to bring your mind back under control and stop it running away. All we have to do is distract our mind from its emotional focus, by centring or grounding ourselves. Over the previous weeks, you have been practising various methods to distract your mind. Hopefully you will have found at least one method that works for you. This becomes the method that you can use to centre yourself when things begin to get uncomfortable emotionally.

Go back over your notes from the mind distraction exercises to remind yourself which ones worked best for you.

Daily tasks

The next time you find yourself becoming emotional in response to a situation, distract your mind using the method that works best for you. For example, this could be an awareness of the pressure of your body weight on the soles of your feet, or you might start to follow your breath in and out. Other people will be completely unaware of what you are doing. For this to work effectively, you need to use it when you notice the very first signs of the emotion stirring, for example your heart beat may begin to quicken when you meet someone who stirs anger within you.

Now PAUSE Reading

Complete a week of being aware of unwanted emotions before you resume reading.

Resume reading

Personal notes ✎

What worked well for you?

What did you discover?

How did this make you feel?

Second week   *Weaken unwanted emotions*

Most of us suffer from one or more emotions that just flare up, seemingly out of our control. Whichever of your emotions that distress you, there is a simple technique that weakens the emotion. Become aware of your emotions as they happen and feel the physical affects that they cause in your body. This is almost like 'tasting' the effect of the emotion. Our unwanted strong emotions do not like to be closely observed by us and this has the gentle effect over time of diminishing those emotions.

It's ok to have strong emotions; they are proof that you are very much alive, but some are better than others.

Daily tasks

Do you find yourself getting angry, sometimes over the smallest of things? Controlling your anger is no easy task, but a simple step that you can take is to develop an awareness of when it occurs. The next time anger begins to well up inside you, just take a moment to become aware of what is happening. Don't question the cause or reason for it, just watch and observe your body, heart rate, breathing, temperature and the tension in your stomach. Every time that you become aware what is happening the intensity of the anger will diminish just a little.

The same approach applies to sadness, if you find the veil of sadness coming over you for no apparent reason. One minute everything is ok, and then suddenly your mood changes and you feel burdened with a great weight, doing the simplest of tasks becomes more difficult. It's a strange feeling like the whole world has changed around you as you are weighed down with melancholy. Good thoughts are difficult to force through, your heart beats heavier in your chest. Then some time later it quietly lifts unnoticed as if it were never there. Just watch and observe how it feels physically.

Fear is another emotion that plagues many of us, causing tightness in the chest, faster heart rate, faster breathing and a sick feeling in your stomach. At its very worst it can be completely debilitating, you literally become frozen in fear. When you experience fear, feel your fear, notice its effect upon you physically, how it begins and how it eventually leaves you. Your fear does not like to be observed and is a little shy, so every time you feel your fear and watch it, you will weaken its intensity.

You can apply this technique to any powerful unwanted emotions that you may experience. Concentrate on the physical symptoms in your body that the emotion stirs within you. And face your emotion head on.

Now PAUSE Reading

Complete a week of weakening unwanted emotions before you resume reading.

Resume reading

Personal notes

What worked well for you?

What did you discover?

How did this make you feel?

Third week *Letting go*

Often we become irritated by the actions of others, whose careless behaviour can have a long lasting impact upon our emotions.

I become agitated when someone else behaves in a way that is unacceptable to me, for example if they pull their car out in front of mine without looking, causing me to brake heavily. I then get angry and rattled about the whole thing.

Sequence	My view	Their view
1	Driving along happily	Approaching junction. I'm late collecting the kids from school and my mind is dealing with lots of things. I need to get a move on. I can drive quickly because it is well within my abilities.
2	Car pulls out in front of me, I brake heavily to avoid hitting car	I will just quickly pull out well ahead of this oncoming slow car.
3	I'm angry; they have just cut me up, having quite clearly seen me.	Still thinking about the kids
4	I now begin to behave aggressively, possibly dangerously towards other drivers	Not aware that anything has happened
5	This has put me in an agitated mood for the rest of the day.	Relieved, arrived on time to collect the kids.

So all that has happened here is that I have wound myself up and the 'offender' is totally unaware of the whole thing. The only person to suffer here is me.

There is another way of viewing this:

Letting go is an approach that you could take here. One way of dealing with incidents like this is simply to let go and walk away from incidents where other people do not behave as you expect them to. We all have a completely different view of life based upon a lifetime of experiences from our parents, teachers, media and friends. You can't change other people's lifetime of experiences to align with your belief and values. So other people will never experience things the same way as you. When your expectations are not met by others, just let it go and move on. You can be sure that it isn't troubling them.

This can be very frustrating with family and friends because issues keep coming up time and again with them not seeing things as you do.

Daily tasks

The next time you find yourself getting agitated over the actions of someone else, just become aware of your reaction. Then just carry on and be angry/agitated or whatever your reaction is.

After this has happened a few times, try to just let it go. I know that this sounds easier said than done, but just move on to what you were thinking about or doing prior to the annoyance occurring.

Now PAUSE Reading

Complete a week of letting go before you resume reading.

Resume reading

Personal notes

What worked well for you?

What did you discover?

How did this make you feel?

Fourth week   How do I feel?

An interesting approach to becoming more in touch with your emotions is to get into the regular habit of simply asking yourself how you feel about things at any given time. The more often you check your feelings, you begin to develop an awareness of how you are responding to life. It begins to give you more control over your emotions so you are swept along less by them.

Daily tasks

Try snatching regular moments during the day to reflect on how you feel. It may only take a few seconds, don't think about it but experience how you feel emotionally at this moment. You can do this at any time, whilst making a cup of coffee or walking down the street. Just take a deep breath and relax and experience your emotions. How do you feel?

It is also good to get into the habit of asking yourself how you feel when you react strongly towards something.

Now PAUSE Reading

Complete a week of asking how you feel before you resume reading.

Resume reading

Personal notes ✎

What worked well for you?

What did you discover?

How did this make you feel?

Workshop – calm your emotions

Summary

Over the past few weeks we have looked at calming our unwanted emotions by letting go of things that we have no control over and learning to 'taste' unpleasant emotions.

Workshop activity

During your next visit to the supermarket (or your workshop of choice) we are going to practice some of the techniques from this chapter. But first glance back over the previous weeks to remind yourself of the different approaches that you have explored.

Allow more time for your visit and then perform your shopping in the usual way. Apply all those techniques that you found helpful from previous chapters.

Distract your mind from its chatter by becoming more aware of the world around you.
Rest your mind by providing opportunities to slow down and force idle breaks into your schedule.
Emotional awareness through listening to others, and your own thoughts and emotions.

This time pay special attention to the following:

Centring   Have a go at calming emotions as they begin by distracting your mind.

Emotions   If you experience a moment of powerful emotion such as fear, notice how it 'tastes' and feel the physical effect it has.

Let go   Someone says or does something that provokes you, just let it go.

How do I feel Keep asking yourself.

Now *PAUSE* Reading

Visit your supermarket for your normal weekly shopping, this time set off earlier and allow more time for your shopping. Try to calm your challenging emotions. Then resume reading.

Resume reading

Personal notes ✎

What worked well for you?

What did you discover?

How did this make you feel?

Workshop review

Now you have slowed down your busy mind and created opportunities to observe your thoughts and emotions in an impartial way. This has opened the way to start looking at our more powerful unwanted emotions, and exploring approaches that calm them a little.

What can you take from this chapter?

The simple knack of managing our strong emotions is to become aware of them as and when they flare up. To feel and experience the physical effect on your body. These emotions are almost 'shy', the more you observe them impartially; the weaker they will become. This is a very slow gentle process but the big emotions will gradually calm down.

Chapter 7   Playtime for the mind

Most of the exercises in the book have been about calming your mind and simply making each day a little easier, now we are going to have some fun and try some activities that soften your thinking and allow your mind to expand a little.

First week   Drawing

If you are thinking –oh no drawing is not for me, I can't draw - then this week is for you. When we draw as children we do not concern ourselves with the accuracy or style of our drawings we just get on and enjoy the activity. As we get older we avoid drawing at all costs just in case we become embarrassed by the results. Unless of course you have a natural talent, then you already understand the simple pleasure in drawing. If you can get over the need to judge the result, then it can be a very relaxing activity.

Grab a pen and paper and draw something – anything; an item of furniture in the room or copy another picture. Perspective and all the 'rules' of drawing do not matter here, what we are interested in doing is expressing yourself on paper in your own unique way. The result does not have to look exactly like your subject; it can take whatever form you like. The best advice is not to become involved in the techniques of drawing but in the process of doing it, just let it flow and do not judge it, don't try to 'get it right'.

Daily tasks

Try to grab a moment each day to do a quick sketch, take as much time as you can spare. Avoid sharing your results with anyone and resist the temptation to criticise the quality of your work. Just enjoy quietly expressing yourself.

Now PAUSE Reading

Complete a week of drawings before you resume reading.

Resume reading

Personal notes 🖊

What worked well for you?

What did you discover?

How did this make you feel?

Second week   *Smile*

We sometimes forget the simple pleasure in having a smile returned, especially so from a stranger. This week we are going to interact more with the people around us, and acknowledge them with one currency that works the world over, the smile.

Just for now practice the odd smile at yourself when you pass a mirror. How does that feel?

Daily tasks

Take any opportunities that arise to acknowledge the presence of others with a smile, and see what comes of it. Start with people you know, just exchange a smile with them. Then, when the opportunity seems appropriate, exchange a smile with a stranger. It's only for a week, just have a little fun with this exercise. You will be surprised how much brighter the day becomes when someone you do not know returns your smile. And you can be conscious that you have had a similar effect upon them.

Now PAUSE Reading

Complete a week of smiling before you resume reading.

Resume reading

Personal notes ✎

What worked well for you?

What did you discover?

How did this make you feel?

Third week   *Do something pointless*

This week we are going to try a small activity each day that is completely pointless. This can be so liberating when we fill our days with an endless succession of activities and things to do, completing one task only to move onto the next, in a rush to make best use of our time. This week we will waste some of our time. Let's have a quiet laugh with ourselves and try some activities that are completely pointless but calming.

Daily tasks

Every day try to do at least one pointless activity, the more the better. Enjoy being a rebel and wasting some time, its fun and good for your mind.

Stuck for an idea? How about:
- ❖ Catching leaves falling from trees in the Autumn
- ❖ Learning the names of trees
- ❖ Watching shadows
- ❖ Squeezing plastic bubble wrap
- ❖ Doodling with a pen on paper
- ❖ Skimming stones on a lake
- ❖ Watching a river flowing
- ❖ Leaning on walls
- ❖ Building a house of playing cards
- ❖ Reading gravestones

Now PAUSE Reading

Complete a week of pointless activities before you resume reading.

Resume reading

Personal notes 🖊

What worked well for you?

What did you discover?

How did this make you feel?

Fourth week   *Switch off the TV*

The programmes broadcast on the TV tend to be highly stimulating both visually and audibly. Your mind is bombarded with information that it tries to interpret and make sense of. Viewing the TV is presented as a leisure activity, this may be true for your physical body, but this is not the case for your mind which is working hard to process all the moving images and sounds. Since the whole point of the exercises in this book are to lessen the load upon your mind, reducing your TV viewing time eases the work load upon your mind.

Do you watch TV before going to sleep, but have problems sleeping? Stimulating your brain with moving images before going to sleep can agitate your mind and lead to restless sleep.

Are you ready for a real challenge? Do you think that you can cope without watching the TV for a week? If so read on.

I do understand that many of us get locked into watching a series of programmes, so you are allowed to record them and catch up later.

The point of this exercise is not to torture yourself, by depriving yourself of one of the pleasures in your life. So what we want to do now is consider what activities you would like to do if you had lots of time to spare, such as read a book, listen to some great music or be creative and do some craft. Make a list of any activities that you would like to do if only you had the luxury of free time. Ideally we are looking for those more creative activities, which just seem so minor and unimportant and get overlooked in your life. You could even learn a new language, sing or play an instrument. The possibilities are endless.

You may need to get yourself organised before you can start, and acquire any necessary items for your activities.

Daily tasks

Instead of watching the TV at the usual time, try an activity from your list of creative things you would like to do. Work through your list of wishes until you find something that you really enjoy, and then stick with it.

Now PAUSE Reading

Complete a week free from TV engaging in creative activities before you resume reading.

Resume reading

Personal notes ✎

What worked well for you?

What did you discover?

How did this make you feel?

End of week review

Did you rise to the challenge? Have you found an enjoyable activity that could replace some of your viewing time?

The long term knack to reducing your TV viewing hours is very simple. Don't bother watching the first episode of any new series. This is how we are hooked into watching hours of programmes for months to come. If you don't even begin to watch the next 'must see' series then you don't actually feel that you are missing anything. It can feel liberating when you give up that TV series that you have been watching for years, and find that after a few weeks you hardly miss it now that you are learning more interesting skills and crafts for yourself.

Fifth week   *Laughter*

Laughter is great medicine for a troubled mind; one minute of laughing can have the same effect as thirty minutes of relaxation training, so this is a great way to pack some relaxation into a busy schedule. Laughter is also very good exercise for your body, giving all your abdominal muscles a workout. As an added bonus opiates are released by the brain during laughter which has the effect of making you feel good.

Daily tasks

Your challenge this week is to look for opportunities to have a laugh. Begin by laughing at yourself more; seek out situations which will make you laugh, for example, choose comedies on TV rather than dramas this week. Get into the habit of training yourself to notice funny things in your daily life. Look for the absurd things in your surroundings. Laughter has the wonderful effect of being infectious in your fellow human beings and blocks unwanted thoughts from your mind.

Now PAUSE Reading

Complete a week of finding opportunities to laugh before you resume reading.

Resume reading

Personal notes

What worked well for you?

What did you discover?

How did this make you feel?

Sixth week   *Take a break from reading*

If you spend some of your leisure time reading then this can be very challenging. By reading I include everything such as newspapers, magazines and books. As with last week's exercise this gives you an opportunity to do something new with the extra time available.

Daily tasks

Instead of reading at the usual time, continue with the activity from your list of nice things you would like that you enjoyed last week, or try a new one. The most important thing is that it must at least be as enjoyable as reading.

Now PAUSE Reading

Complete a week free from reading before you resume reading.

Resume reading

Personal notes ✎

What worked well for you?

What did you discover?

How did this make you feel?

Seventh week   *Try something different*

It is very easy to live your life with that feeling of 'I wish I had done this or that', with a nagging feeling of regret hanging over us. When opportunities arise to do something that you would really like to do, it is very easy for your thinking mind to talk yourself out it. So this week we are going to have a go at overcoming our natural reluctance to do something that you really fancy.

Daily tasks

Every day do something different, it does not need to be a grand gesture, just a small personal thing, which is different from your normal routine. If you walk from one place to another, just take a slightly different route. Walk into that public building that you have never ventured into before. Browse the art gallery or museum, even if it's only for a few minutes. Just do something very small that interests you but has very little impact upon the routine of your day. Try and keep a gentle forward momentum going every week, slowly shifting your routines in the direction of something more pleasurable.

Now PAUSE Reading

Complete a week of new activities before you resume reading.

Resume reading

Personal notes ✏

What worked well for you?

What did you discover?

How did this make you feel?

End of week review

Now you know how it feels to bring some changes into your life, why not try to keep this going and make small changes a part of your life. If in an earlier weeks exercise, you observed that you had reoccurring regretful thoughts from the past about not trying something, now may be a chance to break that thought by doing something you missed.

Workshop – play time

Summary

Calm comes not just through serious exercises but also by being more playful, over the past few weeks we have explored some lighter activities for your mind. This will just add to the calm foundations that you have already created.

Workshop activity

During your next visit to the supermarket (or your workshop of choice) we are going to practice some of the techniques from this chapter. But first glance back over the previous weeks to remind yourself of the different approaches that you have explored.

Allow more time for your visit and then perform your shopping in the usual way and apply all those techniques that you found helpful from previous chapters.

Distract your mind from its chatter by becoming more aware of the world around you.

Rest your mind by providing opportunities to slow down and force idle breaks into your schedule.

Emotional awareness by listening to others and your own thoughts and emotions.

Emotional calming by learning to let go and feeling the physical effects of strong emotions.

This time pay special attention to the following:

Smile   If it is appropriate, smile at the staff or customers.

Laughing	Look for opportunities for a laugh. Read some comedy cards or browse the comics.
Pointless	Try a pointless but interesting activity. For example reading labels to discover where in the world all your food comes from.
Different	Do something you would not normally do. For example walk around the aisles in a different order or try a new fruit.

Now PAUSE Reading

Visit your supermarket for your normal weekly shopping, this time set off earlier and allow more time for your shopping. Have some fun. Then resume reading.

Resume reading

Personal notes ✏

What worked well for you?

What did you discover?

How did this make you feel?

Workshop review

Now you have slowed down your busy mind and calmed some of your emotions we have created some space to have some fun. This will in turn generate further calm in your life.

What can you take from this chapter?

Many of the techniques for bringing calm into your life can be fun, the knack is remembering amidst all the demands of daily life to be a little lighter in your approach to the day.

Chapter 8   Review

If you have successfully worked through these exercises, then I congratulate you on your efforts.

Did anything work for you?

I do hope that you have enjoyed practicing the various techniques. This isn't about effort or doing long hours of tough exercises. It's about discovering a few techniques that feel right for you and that will fit comfortably into your lifestyle.

Calm comes slowly

Quietening our busy mind and calming our emotions does not come quickly, but slowly through the daily application of some of the techniques that we have used. The key to successfully achieving stillness in your mind is to apply the methods that you have learnt to your daily routine, and then with each passing month you will become calmer.

Review and skim through all the previous chapters, was there anything that particularly worked for you and gave you a sense of calm or made you feel more in touch with yourself? If anything worked for you why not make it a part of your daily life. Get into the habit of snatching moments during the day to have a reality check and acknowledge your feelings.

Distracting your busy mind

Many of the excises for distracting your mind are simply about bringing your awareness into the here and now. When you do this, your mind is relieved of its chatter providing a brief respite from the endless thinking.

Observe your thoughts

Observing your unwanted thoughts as they occur and reflecting on the feelings that they generate, has the very surprising effect of gently weakening the physical effect that they have on you. Powerful unwanted emotions behave as if they are shy, and when closely observed will shrink away. But if left unobserved, they can grow into a monster which can debilitate you.

Gaining some emotional control

Now you are familiar with observing your emotions, the early signs of an unwanted emotion will become clear. By catching them early you have the opportunity to distract your mind using one of the distraction techniques that work well for you, for example feeling the floor under your feet, or following your breathing. This distraction can soften your emotions.

Keep a Journal

Writing a journal or diary brings many benefits and is a convenient, private way of offloading your thoughts and frustrations. You could make journal writing part of your daily routine, or just update it as and when you feel the need. I have now kept a journal for years and can go for weeks at a time without making an entry. Your journal becomes a convenient refuge to record thoughts and feelings not only when there is turbulence in your life, but also to record the good things that happen too. I make it a special ritual; using an old fashioned fountain ink pen.

Frame your days

It is also helpful to create a daily routine, perhaps first thing in the morning when you rise, or last thing at night, depending on whether you are a morning or evening sort of person. Having simple daily rituals is a nice way to frame your day. Every morning I begin the day with some gentle Tai Chi style moves that I made up, then a few simple stretches and finish with some active breathing. I then end the day just before falling asleep by reflecting upon all the pleasant aspects of the day (No matter how bad my day has been!) and look forward to how I want things to turn out the following day. This all creates a nice calming routine to frame every day.

Play time

Try to make some time in your life for giving your mind some light relief, no matter how much of a waste of time it may at first appear.

Chapter 9   What next?

If you have derived any benefits from this book, then why not try other books that could be helpful to your life. A great place to start is your local public library or bookstore; they have some wonderful books on Mind and Body. There are many alternative approaches to finding an easier way of living, many cost nothing to try. Just go with an open mind and see what books appeal to you. You never know where the adventure may take you.

The biggest benefit which comes from feeling calmer is experiencing less stress which can lead to a longer healthier life.

May you be blessed with discovering a calmer life,

Neale

Reminder cards

The key to achieving calm is to get into the habit of carrying out the tasks on a regular basis. One of the difficulties of incorporating the tasks into your daily life is remembering to do them during the first few weeks. Once you are in the habit of completing the tasks, you will no longer need these visual reminders.

You could either make your own calming pictures or cut out the images from the flowing page. Leave the reminders in places that you will discover during your normal working day. For example your wallet, purse, bathroom cabinet or perhaps in a draw. When you see the cards use them as reminder for you to carry out your task.

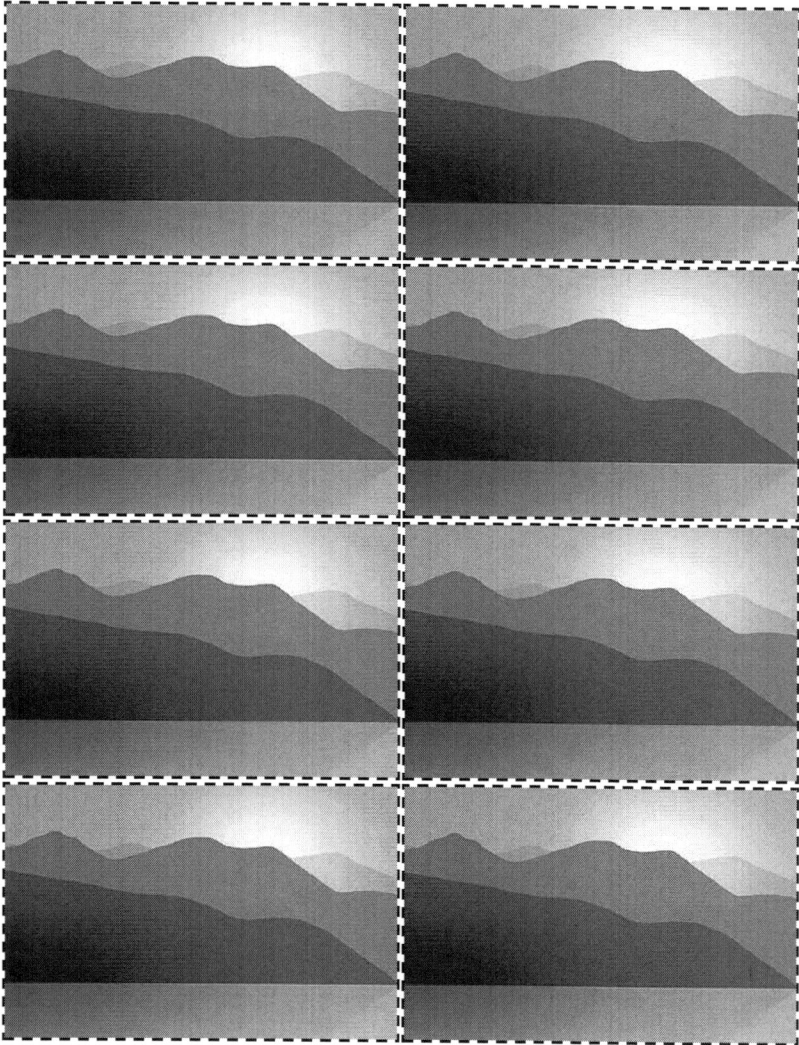

✂ Cut out reminder cards ✂

Blank page

About the author

Born in the sixties, I spent my childhood exploring the countryside of the Peak District. My career developed into almost 30 years as a professional engineer and manager, designing and developing new high technology products.

During this period I became increasingly 'busy' with a hectic career and family life. Feeling the pressure I tried to achieve calm in my life through meditation and visualisation etc, but these failed to defeat my chattering mind. I have trained as a Reiki healer and read many of the classic mind and body books, thoroughly enjoying them but not getting very far in terms of personal calm from any individual book. The outcome was that I developed a 'toolkit' of simple helpful techniques, which could be squeezed into a busy schedule.

After training with the Samaritans* to become a listening volunteer; this led to the realisation that most people are struggling with chattering minds and emotional problems. The outcome was this book in an attempt to share my experience of calming techniques with other busy stressed people.

Working as a life coach, I now teach people how to live happier lives. For my day job, I work at the University of Sheffield developing new relationships with the business world. I live in the Peak District with my wife and a menagerie of animals, where we grow as much food as our English weather allows.

*The Samaritans are an independent charity that offers confidential non-judgemental emotional support, 24 hours a day for people who are experiencing feelings of distress or despair.

Further information

Visit my website at **www.nealedaniel.com** for downloads, links to my blogs and information about courses and other books.

Contact me by email neale@nealedaniel.com